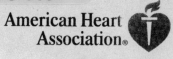

American Heart
Association®

*Learn and Live*_{SM}

Low-Fat
favorite recipes

Featuring Recipes from the *American Heart
Association Low-Fat, Low-Cholesterol
Cookbook, Second Edition*

Clarkson Potter/Publishers
New York

Published by Clarkson Potter/Publishers, New York, New York. Member of the Crown Publishing Group.

Random House, Inc. New York, Toronto, London, Sydney, Auckland
www.randomhouse.com

CLARKSON N. POTTER is a trademark and POTTER and colophon are registered trademarks of Random House, Inc.

All recipes were previously published in the *American Heart Association Low-Fat, Low-Cholesterol Cookbook*, by Times Books, a division of Random House, Inc., in 1989 and 1997.

Printed in the United States of America

ISBN 0-609-89955-4

10

First Edition

CONTENTS

AMERICAN HEART ASSOCIATION DIETARY GUIDELINES

Whether your menu contains exotic ethnic cuisines or traditional all-American favorites, eating for a healthy heart is universal. The American Heart Association recommends the following dietary guidelines for all healthy people over age two. These guidelines can help you reduce blood cholesterol and prevent or control high blood pressure.

AMERICAN HEART ASSOCIATION DIETARY GUIDELINES

- Choose a balanced diet with foods from all major food groups, emphasizing fruits, vegetables, and grains.
- Eat at least 5 servings of fruits and vegetables daily.
- Eat at least 6 servings of grain products daily.
- Eat at least 2 servings of fish per week.
- Include fat-free and low-fat dairy products, legumes, poultry, and lean meats.
- Avoid excess intake of calories, especially those in sugar.
- Maintain a level of physical activity to achieve fitness and to balance calories consumed with calories spent.
- Maintain a healthy body weight.

- Limit your daily cholesterol intake to 300 milligrams (mg). If you are at risk for heart disease, limit your cholesterol to 200 mg per day.
- Limit foods with a high content of saturated fat, trans fat, or cholesterol, such as full-fat milk products, fatty meats, tropical oils, partially hydrogenated vegetable oils, and egg yolks.
- Limit sodium intake to 2,400 mg per day.
- If you drink, limit alcohol consumption to no more than one drink per day for women and two drinks per day for men.

HOW TO FOLLOW THE AMERICAN HEART ASSOCIATION DIETARY GUIDELINES

To stay young at heart, it helps to learn how to create a low-fat, heart-healthy eating plan. Take a look at this breakdown of the nutrients you consume on a daily basis. It will show you the potholes on the road to success, and it will help you make smart choices in each category. We've also included some tips on eating a balanced diet and the importance of getting regular exercise.

Fat

There are three main types of fat in the foods you eat: saturated, trans, and unsaturated. Eating too much fat, especially saturated or trans fat, is not healthful.

Saturated fats are found in meat, poultry, lard, butter, and coconut, palm, and palm kernel oils.

Trans fats are found in commercial products that contain partially hydrogenated vegetable oils. These include vegetable shortenings, stick margarines, and baked goods.

Unsaturated fats include

- Polyunsaturated, found in walnuts, corn oil, safflower oil, and fish
- Monounsaturated, found in olives, olive oil, canola oil, peanut oil, and avocados

Cholesterol

Excess cholesterol and other substances accumulate on the inner walls of your arteries and clog them, which can lead to a heart attack. Not all cholesterol comes from your diet—your body also produces it. That's why it's a good idea to eat less than 300 milligrams of cholesterol a day. Watch out for foods such as egg yolks, organ meats, cream, and cheese. Remember: Dietary cholesterol comes only from animals. Vegetable-based foods contain no cholesterol, although they may contain fat.

Carbohydrates

Think complex. If you eat more complex-carbohydrate foods (such as fruits and vegetables, grains, potatoes, whole-grain breads, rice, and pastas), you'll probably eat less fat. Be sure to leave off the butter and the fatty sauces that simply add fat to these healthful foods.

Protein

Protein is considered your body's construction material. It is the main source for growth and tissue repair. But very little protein is needed to do the job. The fact is, most of us eat about twice as much protein as we need. Some excellent low-fat protein choices are lean meats, poultry, seafood, and nonfat and low-fat dairy products. Other good choices include dried beans, grains, and seeds.

Sodium

Sodium is vital in helping your body maintain a balance of fluids. The Association's recommended guideline of no more than 2,400 milligrams of sodium per day applies to most adolescents and adults. If you have high blood pressure or a history of it in your family, however, your doctor may recommend less sodium. Examples of high-sodium foods are salt (which is about half sodium), soy sauce, Worcestershire sauce, pickles, and canned soups.

Alcohol

Alcohol has no nutritional value. It contains only calories with no nutrients. Too much alcohol can lead to high blood pressure and an increased risk of stroke. Although wine and beer play a large role in certain ethnic cuisines, you can substitute nonalcoholic versions of these beverages in cooking.

Calories

Calories measure energy—the energy your body uses and the energy in the foods you eat. You need a certain number of calories to support body functions, such as breathing, digestion, and physical activity. If you consume more calories than your body needs, you gain weight. If you eat fewer calories than your body needs, you lose weight. So, naturally, if you eat the same number of calories that you burn, you maintain your weight. Your doctor or a dietitian can help you figure out your ideal weight and whether to reduce, increase, or maintain your caloric intake.

Variety

Variety, balance, and moderation are the keys to a well planned, palate-pleasing, and healthful diet. It's important to choose heart-smart foods that you enjoy and that fit into your lifestyle. Why? Because if an eating plan doesn't fit your likes and needs, you probably won't stick to it. The recipes that follow will fit perfectly into your heart-wise eating agenda.

Exercise

Studies show that people who exercise the most, in addition to eating nutritious, low-fat foods, are simply healthier. In fact, people who are fit are less likely to die early from any cause—including cardiovascular disease. Fortunately, you don't have to run marathons to get this protection. Regular moderate exercise will do it.

A good way to get started is by doing moderate activities, such as gardening and light housekeeping. Gradually work up to at least 30 minutes of activity most days of the week. Eventually, you can add low-impact aerobic activities, such as walking, swimming, or biking. That's all it takes. If you are over 40 or if you have any medical problems, check with your doctor before beginning any exercise program.

COOKING FOR
A HEALTHY HEART

Filling your grocery cart with healthful foods is just the beginning of the process. You want the low-fat foods you buy to stay that way until they reach your plate.

Some cooking methods are guaranteed to add loads of fat to any food: Deep-fat frying is a good example. Other cooking methods help retain vitamins and minerals and keep fat and calories to a minimum. These include roasting, baking, broiling, braising, stir-frying, and microwaving.

The idea is to stay away from any cooking method that adds fat or allows food to cook in its own fat. Look for techniques that enhance flavor and preserve nutrients instead. Be miserly when it comes to adding fat and sodium.

Here are a few excellent help-your-heart cooking techniques. Among them, you'll find ways to cook your favorite dishes to perfection so they'll give you the flavor without the fat.

ROASTING

This slow, dry-heat method of cooking creates a delicious product—and keeps fat to a minimum. Simply season the meat, if desired, and place it fat-side-up on a rack in an uncovered roasting pan. Remember to remove as much visible fat as possible from the meat. The rack keeps the meat from sitting in its own fat drippings.

Roast to the desired doneness in a preheated 325° F oven. Cooking at this temperature for the required time increases the fat drip-off and avoids searing the meat, which seals in fat.

Lean meats may require basting with a fat-free liquid such as wine, tomato juice, or lemon juice.

Use a meat thermometer to test for doneness. Insert it in the center of the raw roast so the bulb reaches the thickest part of the meat and does not rest in fat or on bone. When the thermometer shows the desired internal temperature, push it a little deeper into the meat. If the temperature drops, continue cooking until it reaches the correct temperature. If it stays the same, the meat is done.

Time the cooking so the roast is removed from the oven 20 or 30 minutes before serving so the meat can "rest." This ensures that the meat can be carved easily.

BAKING

Baking is another dry-heat form of cooking that's excellent for poultry, fish, and meat. It differs from roasting in that you use a covered container and add some liquid before cooking. The liquid adds flavor and helps keep the meat moist.

BRAISING OR STEWING

Braising is a slow-cooking method that's great for tenderizing tougher cuts of meat. To braise, just brown meat on all sides, using a minimum of vegetable oil or vegetable spray. Then season, add a small amount of liquid (¼ to ½ cup), cover the pan tightly, and simmer. You may also dredge the meat in seasoned flour instead of browning it. For stewing, follow the same directions, but add water to cover.

During cooking, the fat cooks out of the meat. It's a good idea to cook the meat a day ahead, then refrigerate it. After the chilled fat has hardened overnight you can remove it easily before reheating. Also, the flavors of many braised and stewed dishes are improved after refrigerating overnight. Braising is also an excellent way to cook vegetables.

POACHING

Foods are poached by immersion in simmering liquid. It works particularly well with chicken and fish.

Place a single layer of the chicken or fish in a shallow, wide pan and barely cover with liquid. You may use water, water seasoned with spices and herbs, fat-free milk, broth, or a mixture of white wine and water. After cooking, you may reduce the liquid and then thicken it to make a sauce.

STEAMING

Food cooked in a basket over simmering water is just about perfect: It keeps its natural flavor and color and all its vitamins and minerals.

A steam cooker is ideal, but you may also use a steamer basket that fits in a pot with a tight-fitting lid. If you don't have a steamer rack, use anything that will prevent the food from touching the water.

Steaming is great for vegetables. Just bring a small amount of water to a boil (water should be to a depth of about one inch) and then turn the heat to simmer. You may add herbs, spices, or broth to the water for extra flavor. In just a few minutes vegetables will be tender-crisp and ready to eat.

You may even use the liquid left in the pot for soup stock.

STIR-FRYING

This is the Oriental version of sautéing. The idea is to cook food quickly in a minimum amount of oil or broth. The high temperature and the constant stirring keep the food from sticking and burning.

You may use a Chinese wok, designed especially for stir-frying, or a large frying pan. Try stir-frying vegetables and diced chicken or seafood with a tiny bit of peanut oil.

Before you heat the oil in the wok, prepare each food for cooking by dicing or slicing it into small pieces for rapid cooking. Because the hottest area is at the base of the wok, you'll want to cook each food quickly there, then push it up on the side of the wok while you cook the next food.

Use an oil that won't smoke at high temperatures. (Fat that smokes releases undesirable chemicals and won't cook correctly.) Peanut oil, which smokes at 446° F, works best. Stir-frying results in delicious dishes because the hot oil preserves the color, flavor, and crispness of vegetables, and it seals in the natural juices of meats and seafood. When your recipe calls for soy sauce, use the light or low-sodium variety. This helps control the amount of sodium in your diet.

GRILLING OR BROILING

Placing food on a rack and cooking over or under direct heat allows the fat to drip away, either into the coals or into a broiling pan. Either way, much of the fat cooks out.

HOW TO USE
THESE RECIPES

Each recipe includes a nutrient analysis that lists the number of calories and the amount of total fat, saturated fat, polyunsaturated fat, monounsaturated fat, cholesterol, sodium, carbohydrate, fiber, and protein in one serving.

Here are some other important things you should know about the analyses.

- All values are rounded. Because of rounding, the values for saturated, monounsaturated, and polyunsaturated fat don't always add up to the total fat value.
- The analyses do not include optional ingredients or garnishes. If you add any of these, you need to count the calories, saturated fat, sodium, and other nutrients contained in the additions.
- For "acceptable margarine," we used corn oil margarine in the analysis. When shopping, choose margarine that lists liquid vegetable oil as its first ingredient.
- For "acceptable vegetable oil," we used corn oil in the analysis. Other acceptable vegetable oils include canola, olive, and safflower.
- When you buy commercial varieties of canned broth, salsa, low-fat flour tortillas, barbecue sauce,

ketchup, Worcestershire sauce, soy sauce, and steak sauce, read the nutrition labels carefully. If you choose the products with the lowest amounts of sodium, you will come close to our analyses.

- When a choice of ingredients is listed (for example, 1 cup nonfat or low-fat yogurt), we used the first ingredient for the analysis.
- When a recipe calls for an ingredient that may vary in amount (for example, a 2½- to 3-pound chicken), we analyzed the average of the range.
- Meat statistics were based on cooked lean meat with all the visible fat removed. For lean ground beef, we used 90 percent fat free.
- When analyzing marinated meat, poultry, or seafood, we calculated only the amount of marinade absorbed by the food. No similar data is available for marinated vegetables, so we included the total amount of the marinade.
- We don't know how much sodium is removed when rinsing salty foods such as olives, capers, and feta cheese, but we usually suggest rinsing such foods. Rinsing will lower the sodium level that's listed in the nutrient analysis.

Zesty Potato Skins

Serves 8

6 medium red potatoes, baked (about 1¼ pounds)
Vegetable oil spray
½ teaspoon garlic powder
½ teaspoon chili powder
½ teaspoon ground cumin
⅛ teaspoon pepper
1 cup nonfat or low-fat cottage cheese, undrained
    (8 ounces)
½ teaspoon grated lime rind
1½ tablespoons fresh lime juice
1 teaspoon dried chives
¼ teaspoon chili powder
24 slices black olives (4 large)

Preheat oven to 450° F.

Cut each potato in half. Scoop out the center, leaving about ¼ inch of potato on the inside of each skin. Cut skins into quarters. Lightly spray insides of skins with vegetable oil spray.

In a small bowl, combine garlic powder, ½ teaspoon chili powder, cumin, and pepper. Sprinkle mixture evenly on insides of potatoes.

Place skins, skin side down, on a baking sheet. Bake for 15 to 20 minutes, or until lightly browned.

Meanwhile, combine remaining ingredients except olives in a blender or food processor. Process until smooth.

Spoon about 1 teaspoon of the cottage cheese mixture on top of each potato skin and top with a slice of olive.

Calories	50	Total Fat	0 g	Fiber	1 g
Protein	4 g	Saturated	0 g	Sodium	128 mg
Carbohydrate	8 g	Polyunsaturated	0 g		
Cholesterol	0 mg	Monounsaturated	0 g		

Crab Spring Rolls with Peanut Dipping Sauce

Serves 10

SPRING ROLLS
Vegetable oil spray
4 cups shredded cabbage (about 1 pound)
1 medium carrot, shredded
½ cup bean sprouts (about 1 ounce)
2 green onions, thinly sliced
4 ounces nonfat imitation crabmeat, shredded
2 teaspoons rice vinegar
1 teaspoon reduced-sodium soy sauce
10 spring roll wrappers (8 x 8 inches)
White of 1 egg, lightly beaten
Vegetable oil spray

DIPPING SAUCE
3 tablespoons reduced-fat peanut butter
3 tablespoons rice vinegar
2 tablespoons reduced-sodium soy sauce
2 tablespoons water
1 green onion, green part only, thinly sliced
½ teaspoon fragrant toasted sesame oil

Spray a large skillet with vegetable oil spray. Heat over medium-high heat for 1 to 2 minutes. Add the cabbage and cook, stirring occasionally, for 1 to 2 minutes.

Add the carrot, bean sprouts, and green onions and cook for 1 minute, stirring occasionally.

Add the crabmeat, vinegar, and soy sauce and cook until crabmeat is warmed through, about 30 seconds. Remove from heat and refrigerate for at least 30 minutes.

Preheat oven to 400° F.

To assemble spring rolls, place a spring roll wrapper on a flat surface, with one point of the wrapper pointing toward you. Spoon about ⅓ cup of the fillng up the middle of the wrapper. Bring the bottom point of the wrapper over the filling. Lightly brush the two side points of the wrapper with egg white. Bring the side points into the center of the wrapper (wrapper will look like an unsealed envelope). Starting from the bottom, roll the wrapper up to the top point so the filling is enclosed. Lightly brush the top point with egg white and press to make sure the spring roll is sealed. Lightly spray outside of spring roll with vegetable oil spray and place on a baking sheet. Repeat with remaining wrappers.

Bake for 25 to 30 minutes, or until wrapper turns a light golden-brown.

While spring rolls are baking, place all dipping sauce ingredients except green onion in a medium bowl and whisk. Sprinkle dipping sauce with green onion and serve with the spring rolls.

COOK'S TIP

You can assemble spring rolls and keep them in the refrigerator for up to 8 hours before baking or for up to 2 months in the freezer. (Do not thaw before baking.) The dipping sauce will keep for up to 2 days in the refrigerator, the filling for up to 4 days.

COOK'S TIP ON SESAME OIL

Fragrant toasted sesame oil, also called toasted sesame oil or Asian sesame oil, is darker, stronger, and more fragrant than sesame oil. Fragrant toasted sesame oil is widely used in Asian and Indian foods. Because it is so flavorful, you get a lot of taste for just a little fat.

Calories	138	Total Fat	3 g	Fiber	2 g
Protein	7 g	Saturated	0 g	Sodium	300 mg
Carbohydrate	22 g	Polyunsaturated	1 g		
Cholesterol	18 mg	Monounsaturated	1 g		

Tomato, Orange, and Tarragon Soup

Serves 6

1 teaspoon acceptable vegetable oil
12 ounces white or red potatoes, peeled and diced
1 medium yellow or white onion, sliced
3 large tomatoes, chopped (about 1½ pounds)
2 cups low-sodium chicken broth
2 tablespoons chopped fresh tarragon or 2 teaspoons
    dried, crumbled
1 clove garlic, crushed, or ½ teaspoon bottled minced
    garlic
¼ teaspoon salt (optional)
Freshly ground pepper to taste
1 teaspoon grated orange rind
1 cup fresh orange juice (3 to 4 medium oranges)
Fresh tarragon or parsley sprigs (optional)

In a heavy nonstick saucepan, heat oil over medium-high heat. Sauté potatoes and onion for 2 to 3 minutes, or until onion is translucent.

Stir in tomatoes, broth, tarragon, garlic, salt, and pepper. Bring to a boil over high heat. Reduce heat and simmer, covered, for 20 to 25 minutes, or until vegetables are tender.

In a blender or food processor, process soup in small batches until liquefied. Pour through a sieve to remove coarse skins. Discard skins.

Stir orange rind and juice into strained soup. Reheat or serve chilled. Garnish with fresh tarragon.

Calories	111	Total Fat	1 g	Fiber	2 g
Protein	3 g	Saturated	0 g	Sodium	32 mg
Carbohydrate	22 g	Polyunsaturated	1 g		
Cholesterol	0 mg	Monounsaturated	0 g		

Light and Lemony Spinach Soup

Serves 2

2 cups low-sodium chicken broth
2 teaspoons fresh lemon juice
1/4 teaspoon dried thyme, crumbled
1/8 teaspoon salt (optional)
4 leaves spinach or other greens, such as escarole, torn
1 green onion (green part only), thinly sliced

In a 1-quart saucepan, combine broth, lemon juice, thyme, and salt. Bring to a boil over high heat.

Meanwhile, place spinach in bowls.

Pour hot soup over spinach. Top soup with green onion. Serve immediately.

Calories	37	Total Fat	1 g	Fiber	1 g
Protein	4 g	Saturated	0 g	Sodium	88 mg
Carbohydrate	4 g	Polyunsaturated	0 g		
Cholesterol	0 mg	Monounsaturated	0 g		

Warm Mushroom Salad

Serves 4

¼ cup port, sweet red wine, or frozen unsweetened apple
    juice concentrate
3 to 3½ tablespoons balsamic vinegar or rice vinegar
2 tablespoons water
3 cloves garlic, finely minced, or 1½ teaspoons bottled
    minced garlic
12 ounces fresh mushrooms, cut into ¼-inch-thick slices
1 teaspoon light margarine
⅛ teaspoon freshly ground pepper, or to taste
4 leaves Boston lettuce
1 teaspoon chopped fresh parsley

In a nonstick skillet, heat port, vinegar, water, and garlic
over medium-high heat until small bubbles begin to
form.

Add mushrooms and cook, stirring frequently, for 8 to
10 minutes, or until all liquid evaporates.

Add margarine and pepper. Stir to coat evenly.

Arrange mushrooms on lettuce leaves and sprinkle
with parsley. Serve warm.

Calories	29	Total Fat	1 g	Fiber	1 g
Protein	2 g	Saturated	0 g	Sodium	15 mg
Carbohydrate	5 g	Polyunsaturated	0 g		
Cholesterol	0 mg	Monounsaturated	0 g		

Cucumber-Melon Salad
with Raspberry Vinegar

Serves 4

1 medium cucumber
½ large cantaloupe, seeded
1 bunch radishes
¼ cup raspberry vinegar
Freshly ground pepper (optional)
4 lettuce leaves

Partially peel cucumber, leaving some of the dark green to add color. Cut cucumber into bite-size pieces and put them in a medium bowl.

Cut cantaloupe into cubes or use a melon baller to scoop out small balls. Add to cucumber pieces.

Thinly slice the radishes and combine with cucumber and cantaloupe.

Toss salad with vinegar and sprinkle with pepper. Refrigerate, covered, until chilled, about 30 minutes to 1 hour. Serve on individual plates lined with leaf lettuce.

Calories	77	Total Fat	1 g	Fiber	2 g
Protein	2 g	Saturated	0 g	Sodium	21 mg
Carbohydrate	18 g	Polyunsaturated	0 g		
Cholesterol	0 mg	Monounsaturated	0 g		

Fresh Fruit Salad with Poppy Seed and Yogurt Salad Dressing

Serves 6

3 medium oranges
3 cups assorted fresh fruit, cut into bite-size pieces
1 cup nonfat or low-fat lemon yogurt
¼ teaspoon poppy seeds
6 fresh mint sprigs or edible flowers

Cut each orange in half. Cut a thin slice from the bottom of each half so the oranges will sit upright. Remove the flesh from each half. Coarsely chop the flesh and place pieces in a large bowl.

Add other fruit to orange pieces. Stir to combine.

Place each orange "bowl" on a small plate. Place fruit in orange bowls, letting any extra fruit cascade onto the plate.

In a small bowl, whisk together yogurt and poppy seeds, then pour over fruit, using 2 to 3 tablespoons per serving. Top each serving with a sprig of mint or a flower.

Calories	104	Total Fat	0 g	Fiber	3 g
Protein	3 g	Saturated	0 g	Sodium	18 mg
Carbohydrate	25 g	Polyunsaturated	0 g		
Cholesterol	1 mg	Monounsaturated	0 g		

Poached Fish in Asian Broth

Serves 4

BROTH
3 cups low-sodium chicken broth
2 tablespoons dry sherry
2 tablespoons low-sodium soy sauce
2 slices of lemon
3 thin slices fresh gingerroot
⅛ teaspoon cayenne

1 pound orange roughy or other thick, mild fish fillets
5 to 6 green onions (green part only), cut into 1-inch pieces
1 medium red bell pepper, cut into ¼ × 1-inch pieces
1 celery rib, cut into ¼ × 1-inch pieces
½ teaspoon fragrant toasted sesame oil
1 carrot, grated
Freshly ground pepper to taste

In a nonaluminum fish poacher, a wok, or a large skillet, bring broth ingredients to a boil over high heat.

Rinse fish and pat dry with paper towels. Reduce heat and place fish in broth. Add small amount of water, if needed, to just cover fish. Simmer fish in broth for about 10 minutes per inch of thickness at the thickest point, or just until fish is no longer translucent. Do not overcook.

Remove fish with slotted spatulas and place equal portions in 4 soup bowls.

Return liquid to a boil. Add green onions, bell pepper, and celery. Cook 2 to 3 minutes, or until tender-crisp. Discard lemon and gingerroot. Transfer vegetables to soup bowls. Stir sesame oil into broth. Pour into soup bowls. Sprinkle with carrot and pepper.

Calories	203	Total Fat	8 g	Fiber	2 g
Protein	24 g	Saturated	2 g	Sodium	418 mg
Carbohydrate	7 g	Polyunsaturated	2 g		
Cholesterol	77 mg	Monounsaturated	3 g		

Mesquite-Grilled Red Snapper with Gingered Black Bean Salsa

Serves 4

SALSA
Vegetable oil spray
¼ cup chopped onion
¼ cup chopped carrot
1 to 2 jalapeño peppers, chopped*
2 tablespoons peeled and finely chopped gingerroot
2 to 3 cloves garlic, minced, or 1 to 1½ teaspoons bottled minced garlic
15-ounce can black beans, rinsed and drained, reserving 3 tablespoons liquid
¼ teaspoon salt
1 medium tomato, seeded and chopped

1 pound red snapper fillets (about ½ inch thick)

At least 1 hour before cooking, soak 4 to 6 mesquite wood chunks in enough water to cover. Lightly spray grill rack with vegetable oil spray. Set aside.

Prepare grill.

For salsa, spray a medium saucepan with vegetable oil spray. Cook onion, carrot, jalapeño peppers, gingerroot, and garlic over medium-low heat for about 5 minutes, or until onion is tender.

Stir black beans, reserved bean liquid, and salt into onion mixture. Cook over medium-low heat for 1 to 2 minutes, or until heated through.

Stir in tomato.

Drain wood chunks. Place wood chunks directly on medium-hot coals.

---

* Hot chili peppers contain oils that can burn your skin, lips, and eyes. Wear rubber gloves or wash your hands thoroughly with warm, soapy water immediately after handling peppers.

Rinse fish and pat dry with paper towels. Place fish on prepared rack. Grill on an uncovered grill directly over medium-hot coals for 5 minutes. Turn and grill for 5 to 7 minutes, or until fish flakes easily when tested with a fork.

Place fish on serving plates. Serve with salsa.

BROILING DIRECTIONS

Prepare recipe as directed except spray an unheated broiler rack with vegetable oil spray. Place fish on rack and broil 3 to 5 inches from heat for 5 minutes. Turn fish and broil 5 to 7 minutes, or until fish flakes easily when tested with a fork.

Calories	232	Total Fat	2 g	Fiber	6 g
Protein	29 g	Saturated	0 g	Sodium	455 mg
Carbohydrate	25 g	Polyunsaturated	1 g		
Cholesterol	60 mg	Monounsaturated	0 g		

Grilled Catfish
with Mustard-Lemon Sauce

Serves 4

4 small catfish fillets (about 1 pound)
½ teaspoon pepper
Vegetable oil spray

SAUCE
2 cloves garlic, minced, or 1 teaspoon bottled minced
   garlic
1 tablespoon all-purpose flour
1¼ cups fat-free evaporated milk
1 tablespoon Dijon mustard
2 teaspoons finely shredded lemon rind
1 teaspoon chopped fresh basil, thyme, dill weed, parsley,
   or oregano or ¼ teaspoon dried herb

Prepare grill.

Rinse fish and pat dry with paper towels. Sprinkle both sides of fish with pepper. Lightly spray a grill basket or grill rack with vegetable oil spray. Place fish in basket or on rack. Grill fish on uncovered grill directly over medium-hot coals for about 5 minutes per side, or until fish flakes easily when tested with a fork.

Meanwhile, for sauce, spray a small saucepan with vegetable oil spray. Cook garlic over medium heat for 2 minutes, stirring occasionally.

Stir in flour, then add milk all at once, stirring well.

Add mustard and lemon peel. Cook and stir until thickened and bubbly, 3 to 5 minutes. Stir in basil. Cook and stir 1 minute.

Calories	195	Total Fat	2 g	Fiber	0 g
Protein	31 g	Saturated	0 g	Sodium	249 mg
Carbohydrate	12 g	Polyunsaturated	1 g		
Cholesterol	72 mg	Monounsaturated	0 g		

Baked Crabmeat

Serves 5

Vegetable oil spray
1 teaspoon light margarine
¼ cup finely chopped onion
1 pound crabmeat, all cartilage removed
2 tablespoons Dijon mustard
1 teaspoon Worcestershire sauce
Whites of 4 large eggs, stiffly beaten
2 tablespoons grated or shredded Parmesan cheese

Preheat oven to 350° F.

Spray a 9 × 9-inch ovenproof casserole dish with vegetable oil spray. Set aside.

In a small saucepan, melt margarine over medium-high heat. Add onion and sauté for 2 to 3 minutes, or until soft.

Transfer onion to a medium bowl and stir in crabmeat, mustard, and Worcestershire sauce. Gently fold in beaten egg whites. Pour mixture into casserole dish and sprinkle with cheese.

Bake for 25 minutes, or until puffed and lightly browned. Remove from oven and cut into rectangles. Serve immediately.

Calories	120	Total Fat	3 g	Fiber	0 g
Protein	21 g	Saturated	1 g	Sodium	411 mg
Carbohydrate	2 g	Polyunsaturated	1 g		
Cholesterol	86 mg	Monounsaturated	1 g		

Seafood and Lemon Risotto

Serves 4

Vegetable oil spray
1 medium leek, sliced
2 cloves garlic, minced, or 1 teaspoon bottled minced
  garlic
1 cup Arborio rice (about 8 ounces)
2 cups low-sodium chicken broth, divided use
1 cup dry white wine or nonalcoholic white wine
8 ounces bay scallops, rinsed
8 ounces medium shrimp in shells, rinsed, peeled, and
  deveined
3 ounces fresh snow pea pods, trimmed and halved
  crosswise
½ medium red bell pepper, chopped
3 tablespoons grated or shredded Parmesan cheese
2 tablespoons chopped fresh basil or 2 teaspoons dried,
  crumbled
1½ to 2 tablespoons finely shredded lemon rind
Grated or shredded Parmesan cheese (optional)

Spray a medium saucepan with vegetable oil spray. Cook leek and garlic over medium-low heat for about 5 minutes, or until leek is tender.

Add rice. Stir well. Cook for 5 minutes, stirring often.

Add 1½ cups of broth. Bring to a boil over high heat, stirring occasionally. Reduce heat and simmer, uncovered, for 5 minutes, stirring occasionally.

Add remaining ½ cup chicken broth and wine. Increase heat to medium and cook for 5 to 8 minutes, stirring constantly (a small amount of liquid should remain).

Add scallops, shrimp, pea pods, and bell pepper. Cook, stirring constantly, until liquid is almost absorbed, about 5 minutes (rice should be just tender and slightly creamy).

Stir in 3 tablespoons Parmesan, basil, and lemon peel. Heat through. Serve immediately. Serve with additional Parmesan, if desired.

COOK'S TIP ON RISOTTO

For proper consistency, carefully regulate the cooking temperature so the risotto boils lightly, not vigorously. If the liquid is absorbed before the rice reaches the just-tender stage, add more broth, wine, or water, a little at a time. Arborio rice is usually used in risottos, but you can substitute a medium-grain rice if you prefer. It won't be quite as creamy, however.

Calories	294	Total Fat	3 g	Fiber	2 g
Protein	20 g	Saturated	1 g	Sodium	243 mg
Carbohydrate	44 g	Polyunsaturated	1 g		
Cholesterol	65 mg	Monounsaturated	1 g		

Chicken Breasts Stuffed with Ricotta and Goat Cheese

Serves 4

Vegetable oil spray

STUFFING
7 ounces nonfat or low-fat ricotta cheese
2 ounces goat cheese
2 tablespoons chopped fresh parsley or 2 teaspoons
    dried, crumbled
1 tablespoon chopped fresh chives or 1 teaspoon dried

SAUCE
8-ounce can no-salt-added tomato sauce
2 teaspoons salt-free Italian herb seasoning
1 1/2 teaspoons chopped fresh oregano or 1/2 teaspoon
    dried, crumbled
1 clove garlic, minced, or 1/2 teaspoon bottled minced
    garlic
1/4 to 1/2 teaspoon salt
1/8 teaspoon pepper

4 boneless, skinless chicken breast halves (about 4 ounces
    each), all visible fat removed

Preheat oven to 350° F. Spray a 1-quart casserole dish
lightly with vegetable oil spray. Set aside.

In a small bowl, combine the stuffing ingredients. Set
aside.

In another small bowl, combine the sauce ingredients.
Set aside.

Place breasts smooth side up between 2 sheets of plastic wrap. Using a tortilla press or the smooth side of a
meat mallet, lightly flatten the breasts, being careful not
to tear the meat.

Spoon about one quarter of the stuffing lengthwise

down the middle of each breast. Starting with the short end, roll up the breast jelly-roll style. Place the breast in the prepared casserole dish, seam side down (no need to secure with toothpicks). Repeat with the other breasts.

Spoon sauce over breasts. Bake, covered, for 40 to 45 minutes, or until chicken is cooked through.

Calories	235	Total Fat	6 g	Fiber	1 g
Protein	35 g	Saturated	3 g	Sodium	382 mg
Carbohydrate	9 g	Polyunsaturated	1 g		
Cholesterol	75 mg	Monounsaturated	2 g		

Cheese-Herb Chicken Medallions

Serves 6

6 boneless, skinless chicken breast halves (about 4 ounces
   each), all visible fat removed
1 tablespoon finely chopped fresh chives or 1 teaspoon
   dried
1 tablespoon finely chopped fresh basil or 1 teaspoon
   dried, crumbled
¼ teaspoon paprika
Freshly ground pepper to taste
3 ounces nonfat or part-skim mozzarella cheese,
   shredded, preferably chilled (about ⅔ cup)
2 carrots (optional)

Preheat oven to 400° F.

Place breasts on a flat surface. Evenly sprinkle each
breast with chives, basil, paprika, and pepper.

Form cheese into 6 loose balls and place one in the
center of each breast. Roll chicken around cheese, mak-
ing sure the ends are tucked in. Tie each breast with
twine to retain cheese.

Place breasts in an ungreased baking dish. Bake for
15 to 20 minutes, or until chicken has turned white
throughout. Allow chicken to cool for about 10 minutes
before serving.

Meanwhile, prepare carrot curls. Using a potato
peeler, pare carrots lengthwise into long, thin strips and
soak in ice water for at least 10 minutes. Drain and pat
dry.

To serve, cut each breast into ½-inch medallions.
Arrange on a bed of carrot curls.

Calories	158	Total Fat	3 g	Fiber	0 g
Protein	30 g	Saturated	1 g	Sodium	157 mg
Carbohydrate	1 g	Polyunsaturated	1 g		
Cholesterol	62 mg	Monounsaturated	1 g		

Garlic Chicken Fillets
in Balsamic Vinegar

Serves 8

8 boneless, skinless chicken breast halves (about 4 ounces
    each), all visible fat removed
½ cup all-purpose flour
2 teaspoons olive oil
6 to 8 cloves garlic, minced
Vegetable oil spray
1 cup low-sodium chicken broth
⅓ cup balsamic vinegar
Freshly ground pepper to taste
2 tablespoons water
1 tablespoon cornstarch

Dredge breasts in flour; shake off excess.

Heat a large, heavy nonstick skillet over medium-high heat. Add oil and swirl to coat bottom of skillet. When oil is hot, add breasts. Cook on one side for 2 to 3 minutes, or until golden. Add garlic. Spray top side of breasts with vegetable oil spray. Turn breasts and continue cooking about 2 to 3 minutes, or until golden.

Add broth, balsamic vinegar, and pepper. Reduce heat to medium-low and cook, covered, for 5 to 10 minutes, or until chicken is tender. Remove chicken from skillet. Keep warm.

Pour water into a cup. Add cornstarch, stirring until it dissolves. Add to skillet and boil for 1 to 2 minutes, or until thick and smooth. Pour sauce over chicken.

Calories	183	Total Fat	4 g	Fiber	0 g
Protein	26 g	Saturated	1 g	Sodium	65 mg
Carbohydrate	9 g	Polyunsaturated	1 g		
Cholesterol	62 mg	Monounsaturated	2 g		

Thai Chicken with Basil and Vegetables

Serves 4

SAUCE
2 tablespoons low-sodium chicken broth or water
2 teaspoons fish sauce
2 teaspoons sugar
1 teaspoon reduced-sodium soy sauce

1 pound boneless, skinless chicken breasts, all visible fat
    removed
1 teaspoon acceptable vegetable oil
2 cloves garlic, minced, or 1 teaspoon bottled minced garlic
1 serrano pepper, seeded and chopped (optional)
2 cups broccoli florets (about 4 ounces)
2 carrots, cut into very thin strips
4 green onions, cut into 1-inch pieces
¼ cup firmly packed fresh basil leaves
2 cups cooked rice, jasmine preferred

In a small bowl, combine sauce ingredients. Set aside.

Thinly slice breasts. Set aside.

Heat a wok or large skillet over medium-high heat. Add oil and swirl to cover bottom of wok. Add garlic and serrano pepper. Cook for 10 to 15 seconds.

Add chicken and stir-fry for 3 to 4 minutes, or until chicken is no longer pink in the center.

Add the broccoli, carrots, and green onions and stir-fry for 2 to 3 minutes, or until vegetables are tender-crisp.

Add the reserved sauce mixture and basil. Stir-fry for 1 minute, or until warm. Serve over rice.

Calories	290	Total Fat	5 g	Fiber	3 g
Protein	29 g	Saturated	1 g	Sodium	313 mg
Carbohydrate	32 g	Polyunsaturated	2 g		
Cholesterol	62 mg	Monounsaturated	1 g		

Asian Grilled Chicken

Serves 6

MARINADE

¼ cup honey
3 tablespoons red wine vinegar
¼ cup low-sodium soy sauce
1 clove garlic, minced, or ½ teaspoon bottled minced garlic
2 tablespoons finely chopped fresh parsley
2 teaspoons grated fresh gingerroot or 1 teaspoon ground
    ginger
½ teaspoon freshly ground pepper

6 chicken breasts (about 3½ to 4 pounds), skinned, all
    visible fat removed

In a large bowl, combine all marinade ingredients and
mix well.

Add chicken to marinade and turn to coat all pieces.
Cover and refrigerate for at least 2 hours, turning occasionally.

GRILLING METHOD

Place chicken 6 inches from white-hot coals. Brushing
pieces with marinade and turning them frequently, grill
for 30 to 45 minutes, or until chicken is cooked through.

BROILING METHOD

Preheat broiler. Arrange chicken pieces on baking sheet
and place 5 inches from heat. Brushing pieces with
marinade and turning them frequently, broil for 25 to
30 minutes, or until chicken is cooked through.

Calories	142	Total Fat	3 g	Fiber	0 g
Protein	26 g	Saturated	1 g	Sodium	93 mg
Carbohydrate	0 g	Polyunsaturated	1 g		
Cholesterol	66 mg	Monounsaturated	1 g		

Marinated Steak

Serves 6

1 to 1 ½ pounds flank steak, all visible fat removed

MARINADE
½ cup dry red wine, nonalcoholic red wine, or
    low-sodium beef broth
3 tablespoons minced fresh parsley
3 tablespoons tarragon vinegar or wine vinegar
1 teaspoon acceptable vegetable oil
1 tablespoon chopped fresh oregano
1 tablespoon chopped fresh tarragon
3 cloves garlic, crushed
1 bay leaf
½ teaspoon freshly ground pepper

Vegetable oil spray
Freshly ground pepper to taste

Place steak in an airtight plastic bag or in a baking dish. In a small nonmetallic bowl, combine marinade ingredients. Pour over steak and turn to coat. Cover and refrigerate for at least 8 hours, turning occasionally.

Preheat broiler. Spray broiler pan with vegetable oil spray.

Remove steak from marinade, pat dry, and sprinkle with pepper. Place meat on prepared broiler pan.

Broil 4 to 6 inches from heat until desired doneness, 3 to 5 minutes on each side for medium-rare. Slice diagonally across the grain into thin slices.

Calories	147	Total Fat	7 g	Fiber	0 g
Protein	20 g	Saturated	3 g	Sodium	48 mg
Carbohydrate	0 g	Polyunsaturated	0 g		
Cholesterol	54 mg	Monounsaturated	3 g		

Peppery Beef
with Blue Cheese Sauce

Serves 4

12 ounces flank steak, all visible fat removed
2 teaspoons coarsely cracked pepper
Vegetable oil spray

SAUCE
1 teaspoon light margarine
1 clove garlic, minced, or ½ teaspoon bottled minced garlic
1 tablespoon all-purpose flour
⅔ cup fat-free milk
2 tablespoons crumbled blue cheese (about ½ ounce)
2 tablespoons finely chopped green onion (1 to 2)
1 tablespoon dry white wine or nonalcoholic white wine
    (optional)

Make 6 shallow crisscross slashes on the meat (3 in each direction). Rub meat with about half the pepper. Make 6 slashes on other side of meat. Rub with remaining pepper.

Lightly spray the unheated rack of a broiler pan with vegetable oil spray. Broil meat 3 to 5 inches from the heat for 5 minutes. Turn and broil 3 to 5 minutes, or until desired doneness.

Meanwhile, for sauce, melt margarine in a small saucepan over medium heat. Add garlic; cook for 1 minute.

Stir in flour, then stir in milk all at once (a whisk works well). Cook and stir until thickened and bubbly, about 5 minutes; cook and stir 1 minute more. Remove from heat. Stir in remaining sauce ingredients.

To serve, thinly slice meat diagonally across the grain. Serve with sauce.

Calories	177	Total Fat	8 g	Fiber	0 g
Protein	21 g	Saturated	3 g	Sodium	136 mg
Carbohydrate	5 g	Polyunsaturated	0 g		
Cholesterol	52 mg	Monounsaturated	3 g		

Ground Beef Ragout

Serves 6

1½ pounds lean ground beef (90 percent lean)
1 large onion, chopped
2 large tomatoes, chopped
8-ounce can no-salt-added tomato sauce
¾ cup dry red wine, nonalcoholic red wine, or water
½ cup water
1 red chili pepper, seeded and chopped (optional)*
1 tablespoon fresh oregano or 1 teaspoon dried,
    crumbled
3 cloves garlic, minced, or 1½ teaspoons bottled minced
    garlic
1 teaspoon chili powder, or to taste
1 teaspoon ground cumin
½ teaspoon salt (optional)
Freshly ground pepper to taste
15-ounce can low-sodium kidney beans, drained
15-ounce can Great Northern, black, or lima beans,
    rinsed and drained
¼ cup chopped fresh parsley

Heat a 3-quart sauté pan or Dutch oven over medium-high heat. Add ground beef and sauté, stirring occasionally, for 4 to 5 minutes, or until meat is no longer pink. Pour beef into a strainer or colander. Rinse under hot water.

Return beef to the pan, add onion, and sauté for 4 to 5 minutes, or until onion is translucent.

Stir in remaining ingredients except beans. Bring mixture to a boil. Reduce heat and simmer, partially covered, for about 45 minutes, stirring occasionally.

---

* Hot chili peppers contain oils that can burn your skin, lips, and eyes. Wear rubber gloves or wash your hands thoroughly with warm, soapy water immediately after handling peppers.

Add beans and simmer for 10 to 15 minutes, or until beans are thoroughly heated. Sprinkle with parsley before serving.

COOK'S TIP

Sometimes a small change makes a big difference. Substitute 1 cup of pearl onions (about 4 ounces) for the chopped onion in this recipe and see what we mean. Add the pearl onions with the wine, water, and other ingredients just after rinsing the cooked beef.

Calories	339	Total Fat	7 g	Fiber	7 g
Protein	36 g	Saturated	2 g	Sodium	84 mg
Carbohydrate	33 g	Polyunsaturated	1 g		
Cholesterol	68 mg	Monounsaturated	3 g		

Pork with
Corn-Cilantro Pesto

Serves 4

Vegetable oil spray
¼ cup Corn-Cilantro Pesto (recipe follows)
1 pound pork tenderloin, all visible fat removed
1 cup Tomato Sauce (recipe follows)

CORN-CILANTRO PESTO (ABOUT ¾ CUP)
1 cup firmly packed cilantro leaves
¼ cup firmly packed parsley leaves
¼ cup grated or shredded Parmesan or Romano cheese
    (about 1 ounce)
⅓ cup canned no-salt-added whole kernel corn, drained
    (about 3 ounces)
2 tablespoons chopped pecans, preferably dry-roasted
1 tablespoon chopped shallot
1 tablespoon fresh lime juice
2 cloves garlic, quartered
¼ teaspoon salt
4 teaspoons olive oil
Fresh lime juice or water (optional)

TOMATO SAUCE (ABOUT 1 CUP)
Vegetable oil spray
½ cup chopped onion (about 1 medium)
1 clove garlic, minced, or 2 teaspoons bottled minced garlic
8-ounce can no-salt-added tomato sauce
¼ teaspoon sugar
¼ teaspoon salt
⅛ teaspoon pepper

Using vegetable oil spray, spray a broiler pan with rack
or a wire rack and a shallow roasting pan.

Prepare pesto in a blender or food processor. Process
cilantro, parsley, Parmesan, corn, pecans, shallot, 1 table-

spoon lime juice, garlic, and salt until well combined, stopping and scraping sides occasionally.

With machine running, gradually add oil. Process until well combined. If the pesto is thicker than you like, add a teaspoon or so of lime juice.

Preheat oven to 425° F.

Butterfly the tenderloin by cutting it lengthwise almost in half. Lay out flat. Cover meat with plastic wrap. Use the flat side of a meat mallet to pound meat to a ¼-inch thickness.

Spread ¼ cup of pesto over cut surface of tenderloin. Roll up tenderloin from one of the short ends and tie in several places with string to secure. (Can be wrapped in plastic wrap at this point and stored in the refrigerator for 4 to 6 hours before cooking.)

Place tenderloin on prepared rack in broiler pan. Roast, uncovered, for 20 minutes, then turn tenderloin over and roast 10 to 20 minutes, or until a meat thermometer registers 160° F. Remove from oven and let stand 5 minutes.

Meanwhile, prepare tomato sauce. Spray a medium saucepan with vegetable oil spray. Add onion and garlic and cook over medium-low heat for about 5 minutes, or until tender.

Stir in remaining sauce ingredients. Bring to a boil over high heat. Reduce heat and simmer, uncovered, for 5 minutes, or until desired consistency.

Cut pork into medallions and serve with sauce.

COOK'S TIP

Tenderloin usually comes packaged in 2 pieces. Wrap the unused piece and refrigerate or freeze for another recipe.

Refrigerate leftover pesto in a small airtight container for up to 1 week or freeze for up to 1 month.

Calories	211	Total Fat	7 g	Fiber	1 g
Protein	28 g	Saturated	2 g	Sodium	295 mg
Carbohydrate	8 g	Polyunsaturated	1 g		
Cholesterol	73 mg	Monounsaturated	4 g		

Spicy Baked Pork Chops

Serves 4

Vegetable oil spray
1 pound boneless pork loin chops, all visible fat removed
Egg substitute equivalent to 1 egg, or 1 egg
2 tablespoons fat-free milk
⅓ cup cornflake crumbs
2 tablespoons cornmeal
½ teaspoon dried marjoram, crumbled
⅛ teaspoon ground pepper
⅛ teaspoon dry mustard
⅛ teaspoon ground ginger
⅛ teaspoon cayenne

Preheat oven to 375° F. Using vegetable oil spray, spray a shallow baking pan large enough to hold pork chops in a single layer. Set aside.

Cut pork chops into 4 portions, if necessary. Set aside.

In a small, shallow bowl such as a soup bowl, combine egg substitute and milk.

In a shallow dish such as a pie pan, combine crumbs, cornmeal, marjoram, pepper, mustard, ginger, and cayenne. Using tongs, dip pork chops in milk mixture, letting excess liquid drip off. Coat both sides of pork chops with crumb mixture. Arrange pork chops in prepared pan.

Bake, uncovered, for 15 minutes. Turn chops with a spatula and bake for 10 minutes, or until chops are tender and slightly pink in center.

Calories	234	Total Fat	9 g	Fiber	1 g
Protein	27 g	Saturated	3 g	Sodium	142 mg
Carbohydrate	11 g	Polyunsaturated	1 g		
Cholesterol	70 mg	Monounsaturated	4 g		

Spinach and Black Bean Enchiladas

Serves 6

8 cups fresh spinach leaves, stemmed (1 pound)
Vegetable oil spray, if needed
15-ounce can black beans, drained and rinsed
½ cup low-sodium salsa
¼ teaspoon ground cumin
¼ teaspoon chili powder
6 6-inch corn tortillas or nonfat or low-fat flour tortillas
½ cup nonfat or low-fat sour cream
1½ to 2 teaspoons fresh lime juice
4 ounces shredded nonfat or low-fat Monterey Jack cheese
    (about 1 cup)
2 Italian plum tomatoes, diced
2 green onions (green and white parts), thinly sliced

In a large pot, bring several quarts of water to a boil.

Add spinach and cook for 1 minute. Drain well. Press out as much liquid as possible.

Preheat oven to 350° F. Spray a large casserole dish with vegetable oil spray.

In a medium bowl, combine spinach, black beans, salsa, cumin, and chili powder. Spoon one fourth of the mixture down the middle of one tortilla. Roll the tortilla around the filling (jelly-roll style). Place tortilla seam side down in a casserole dish. Repeat with remaining tortillas.

Bake enchiladas, uncovered, for 15 minutes.

Meanwhile, combine sour cream and lime juice. Spread over enchiladas. Top with cheese, tomatoes, and green onions and bake for 5 minutes.

Calories	201	Total Fat	1 g	Fiber	9 g
Protein	17 g	Saturated	0 g	Sodium	374 mg
Carbohydrate	34 g	Polyunsaturated	1 g		
Cholesterol	3 mg	Monounsaturated	0 g		

Grilled Portobello Mushrooms
with Couscous and Greens

Serves 4

4 whole portobello mushrooms
4 tablespoons balsamic vinegar
Vegetable oil spray
1/2 cup low-sodium vegetable broth
1/2 cup water
1/4 teaspoon turmeric
2/3 cup couscous
1/4 cup dried cranberries
1/2 teaspoon grated lemon rind
1/4 teaspoon salt
1 teaspoon olive oil
2 cloves garlic
6 ounces fresh collard greens or kale or 8 ounces fresh
    spinach, chopped (about 4 cups)
2 tablespoons water
1 tablespoon light margarine
1/2 red bell pepper, finely chopped

In the top of each mushroom, cut 4 slits, each 2 to 3 inches long and about 1/2 inch deep. Remove stems. Place mushrooms, top side up, in a shallow casserole dish.

Sprinkle mushrooms with half the balsamic vinegar. Lightly spray top side of mushrooms with vegetable oil spray. Turn mushrooms over and sprinkle with remaining vinegar. Lightly spray bottom side with vegetable oil spray. Cover container with plastic wrap and set aside. (Will keep in refrigerator for up to 1 hour.)

Combine vegetable broth, water, and turmeric in a medium saucepan. Bring to a boil over high heat, 2 to 3 minutes.

Stir in the couscous, cranberries, lemon rind, and salt.

·

Remove pan from heat and let stand, covered, for at least 5 minutes, or until time to serve.

Meanwhile, heat a medium saucepan over medium heat. Add oil and swirl to coat bottom of pan. When oil is hot, add garlic. Cook for 1 minute.

Add the collard greens and 2 tablespoons water. Cook, covered, for 2 to 3 minutes, or until greens are tender.

Add the margarine and stir until it melts, about 30 seconds. Remove pan from heat and cover to help retain heat.

Grill mushrooms over medium-hot coals (or medium-high heat if using gas, electric, propane, or stove-top grill) for 2 to 3 minutes on each side.

Place mushrooms stem side up on serving plates. Spoon couscous on top of each mushroom. Spoon greens on top of couscous. Sprinkle with bell pepper. Serve warm.

Calories	208	Total Fat	3 g	Fiber	7 g
Protein	6 g	Saturated	0 g	Sodium	224 mg
Carbohydrate	40 g	Polyunsaturated	1 g		
Cholesterol	0 mg	Monounsaturated	2 g		

Penne and Cannellini Bean Casserole with Sun-Dried Tomatoes

Serves 8

8 ounces dried penne pasta
8 sun-dried tomatoes (not packed in oil) (about 1 ounce)
Vegetable oil spray
1 tablespoon low-sodium vegetable broth
2 shallots, finely chopped
4 ounces asparagus, sliced diagonally into ½-inch pieces
    (about 1 cup)
½ red bell pepper, diced
1 teaspoon dried oregano, crumbled
⅛ teaspoon pepper
15-ounce can cannellini beans, drained and rinsed
½ cup low-sodium vegetable broth
¼ cup fat-free milk
4 ounces shredded part-skim mozzarella cheese (about
    1 cup)
1 tablespoon light margarine, cut into small pieces

Cook pasta according to package directions, omitting salt and oil. Remove pasta with a large slotted spoon and set aside in a medium bowl.

Add tomatoes to the pasta cooking water, turn off heat, and let tomatoes soak for 15 to 20 minutes.

About halfway through soaking time, preheat oven to 350° F. Spray a 2½-quart shallow casserole dish with vegetable oil spray. Set aside.

Heat a nonstick skillet over medium heat. Add 1 tablespoon vegetable broth and shallots and cook for 1 minute.

Stir in asparagus, bell pepper, oregano, and pepper. Cook, stirring occasionally, for 1 to 2 minutes, or until vegetables are tender-crisp. Turn off heat.

Remove tomatoes from soaking liquid, squeeze out

excess liquid, and dice tomatoes. Add them to the vegetables in skillet and stir to combine.

Layer half the cannellini beans, half the pasta, and half the vegetables in prepared casserole dish. Repeat the layers.

Pour the ½ cup vegetable broth and milk over all. Sprinkle evenly with cheese. Arrange margarine pieces over all.

Lightly cover casserole dish with foil. Bake for 20 minutes; uncover and bake for 5 minutes.

Calories	207	Total Fat	4 g	Fiber	5 g
Protein	12 g	Saturated	2 g	Sodium	254 mg
Carbohydrate	32 g	Polyunsaturated	1 g		
Cholesterol	16 mg	Monounsaturated	1 g		

Honey Carrots

Serves 6

1 ½ pounds fresh or no-salt-added frozen baby carrots
½ cup water
1 tablespoon light margarine
2 tablespoons honey
½ tablespoon light brown sugar
2 to 3 tablespoons minced fresh parsley

Rinse and trim fresh carrots.

In a medium saucepan, bring water to a boil over high heat. Add carrots, reduce heat, and simmer, covered, for about 10 minutes, or until tender-crisp. (If using frozen carrots, follow package directions, omitting margarine and salt.) Drain.

In a large nonstick skillet, melt margarine over medium heat.

Add honey, sugar, and carrots. Reduce heat to medium-low and cook, stirring frequently, until carrots are well glazed, 1 to 2 minutes.

Sprinkle with parsley before serving.

Calories	90	Total Fat	2 g	Fiber	4 g
Protein	1 g	Saturated	1 g	Sodium	93 mg
Carbohydrate	18 g	Polyunsaturated	1 g		
Cholesterol	0 mg	Monounsaturated	1 g		

Home-Fried Potatoes

Serves 6

1 tablespoon acceptable vegetable oil
1½ pounds small red potatoes, unpeeled, cooked and
    quartered
2 medium shallots, chopped
1 teaspoon paprika
½ teaspoon dried rosemary, crushed
½ teaspoon dry mustard
¼ teaspoon salt (optional)
Freshly ground black pepper to taste

In a large, heavy nonstick skillet, heat oil over medium-high heat. Sauté potatoes on one side for 3 to 4 minutes.

Turn potatoes, add shallots, and sauté for 3 to 4 minutes.

Stir in remaining ingredients. Cook for 1 to 2 minutes, or until potatoes are tender.

Calories	122	Total Fat	2 g	Fiber	2 g
Protein	2 g	Saturated	0 g	Sodium	8 mg
Carbohydrate	24 g	Polyunsaturated	1 g		
Cholesterol	0 mg	Monounsaturated	1 g		

Red and Green Pilaf

Serves 4

Vegetable oil spray
½ cup chopped onion
⅓ cup chopped green bell pepper
⅓ cup chopped red bell pepper
½ cup brown rice
2 cloves garlic, minced, or 1 teaspoon bottled minced
    garlic
1½ cups low-sodium chicken broth
¼ teaspoon salt
⅛ teaspoon cayenne
1 cup sliced fresh or frozen okra, thawed, or ⅔ cup
    no-salt-added green peas (6 to 8 ounces fresh or 8 to
    10 ounces frozen okra or 3 to 4 ounces peas)
1 medium Italian plum tomato, seeded and chopped

Spray a medium saucepan with vegetable oil spray. Add onion and bell peppers and cook over medium-high heat for 5 minutes, stirring occasionally.

Stir in rice and garlic and cook for 1 minute.

Add broth, salt, and cayenne. Bring to a boil over high heat. Reduce heat and simmer, covered, for 30 minutes.

Stir in okra. Cook, covered, for 5 to 10 minutes, or until rice is tender and liquid is absorbed.

Stir in tomato. Let stand for 5 minutes before serving.

Calories	119	Total Fat	1 g	Fiber	3 g
Protein	4 g	Saturated	0 g	Sodium	173 mg
Carbohydrate	24 g	Polyunsaturated	0 g		
Cholesterol	0 mg	Monounsaturated	0 g		

Ratatouille

Serves 6

1 large eggplant, cut into 1-inch cubes
4 medium zucchini, sliced ½ inch thick
1 teaspoon salt
1 teaspoon olive oil
2 medium onions, sliced
2 medium red, green, or yellow bell peppers, or any
    combination, chopped
2 large tomatoes, chopped
1 tablespoon chopped fresh thyme
1 tablespoon chopped fresh oregano
1 tablespoon chopped fresh basil
2 cloves garlic, minced
Freshly ground pepper to taste

Unless eggplant is very young, remove peel.

Place eggplant and zucchini in a colander, sprinkle with salt, and toss lightly. Allow to drain for at least 30 minutes. Rinse and pat dry with paper towels.

Heat a large, heavy nonstick skillet over medium-high heat. Add oil and swirl to coat bottom of skillet. When oil is hot, add onions. Sauté until translucent, 2 to 3 minutes.

Stir in all ingredients. Reduce heat and simmer, covered, stirring occasionally, for 30 to 45 minutes, or until vegetables are thoroughly cooked. Uncover and cook for 5 minutes to reduce liquid.

Ratatouille is best made a day ahead to allow flavors to blend. Serve warm or cold.

Calories	93	Total Fat	1 g	Fiber	6 g
Protein	3 g	Saturated	0 g	Sodium	370 mg
Carbohydrate	20 g	Polyunsaturated	0 g		
Cholesterol	0 mg	Monounsaturated	1 g		

Gingerbread Pancakes
with Apple-Berry Topping

Serves 4

1 cup all-purpose flour
2 tablespoons sugar
2 teaspoons baking powder
½ teaspoon ground cinnamon
¼ teaspoon ground ginger
¼ teaspoon ground allspice
¾ cup fat-free milk
Egg substitute equivalent to 1 egg, or 1 egg
2 tablespoons molasses
1 tablespoon acceptable vegetable oil
8 ounces light apple pie filling
½ cup boysenberry, blueberry, or strawberry syrup
4 tablespoons dried cranberries (optional)

Preheat nonstick griddle over medium heat.

In a medium bowl, combine flour, sugar, baking powder, cinnamon, ginger, and allspice.

In a small bowl, combine milk, egg substitute, molasses, and vegetable oil.

Pour wet mixture into dry mixture and stir until just combined. (Do not overmix or pancakes will be tough.)

Test griddle by sprinkling a few drops of water on it. If water evaporates quickly, the griddle is ready. Pour about ¼ cup of the batter onto the griddle. Cook for 2 to 3 minutes, or until bubbles appear all over the surface. Flip over, and cook for 2 minutes, or until bottom is golden-brown. Repeat until all of the batter is used.

While pancakes are cooking, heat the apple pie filling in a small saucepan over low heat for 2 to 3 minutes, or until filling is warmed through. Set aside.

To serve, place 2 pancakes on a plate. Spoon about 2 tablespoons of syrup on pancakes. Spread ¼ cup apple pie filling on top and sprinkle with 1 tablespoon dried cranberries. Repeat with remaining pancakes.

Calories	394	Total Fat	4 g	Fiber	2 g
Protein	6 g	Saturated	1 g	Sodium	342 mg
Carbohydrate	87 g	Polyunsaturated	2 g		
Cholesterol	1 mg	Monounsaturated	1 g		

Breakfast Tortilla Wrap

Serves 4

Vegetable oil spray
Egg substitute equivalent to 2 eggs, or 2 eggs
⅛ teaspoon black pepper
4 6-inch nonfat or low-fat flour tortillas or corn tortillas
1 cup fat-free frozen shredded potatoes (about 3 ounces)
½ red bell pepper, diced
¼ cup chopped Canadian bacon (about 1 ounce)
¼ teaspoon salt
⅛ teaspoon black pepper
Vegetable oil spray
1 ounce nonfat or low-fat Cheddar cheese, shredded
     (about ¼ cup)

Preheat oven to 350° F.

Spray a small nonstick skillet with vegetable oil spray. Heat skillet over medium-low heat. Pour egg substitute into skillet and add ⅛ teaspoon black pepper. Cook, stirring occasionally, for 3 to 4 minutes, or until eggs are cooked through. Set aside.

Wrap tortillas in aluminum foil and warm in oven for 5 minutes.

Meanwhile, in a medium bowl, mix potatoes, bell pepper, Canadian bacon, salt, and remaining black pepper.

Spray a medium-size nonstick skillet with vegetable oil spray. Heat over medium-high heat.

Using a rubber scraper, spread potato mixture evenly over the bottom of the skillet. Cook for 6 to 7 minutes on one side, or until potatoes are a light golden-brown. Turn potato mixture over with a spatula and cook for 5 to 6 minutes.

To assemble using flour tortillas, layer ingredients vertically down the middle of a tortilla as follows: one quarter of the scrambled eggs, one quarter of the potato mixture, and one quarter of the cheese. Fold the left third of the tortilla to the center. Roll the bottom edge all the way up to the top. Repeat with remaining tortillas.

To assemble using corn tortillas, layer ingredients horizontally across the middle of each tortilla as described above. Roll like a jelly roll, starting at the bottom. Secure each wrap with a toothpick, if desired.

Serve immediately, keep in an airtight container, or store individually in plastic wrap. To reheat, place 1 or 2 wraps on a microwave-safe plate. Microwave on 100 percent power (high) for 1 to 1½ minutes.

Calories	142	Total Fat	3 g	Fiber	1 g
Protein	9 g	Saturated	1 g	Sodium	281 mg
Carbohydrate	19 g	Polyunsaturated	1 g		
Cholesterol	5 mg	Monounsaturated	1 g		

Berry Sauce

Serves 6, ¼ cup per serving

16-ounce bag frozen unsweetened strawberries,
    raspberries, or other berries
1 teaspoon cornstarch

Defrost berries and puree in a blender or food processor.

Place berry puree and cornstarch in a medium saucepan. Bring to a boil over medium-high heat, stirring frequently. Cook, continuing to stir frequently, until mixture thickens.

Cover and refrigerate. Serve chilled.

Calories	24	Total Fat	0 g	Fiber	2 g
Protein	0 g	Saturated	0 g	Sodium	1 mg
Carbohydrate	6 g	Polyunsaturated	0 g		
Cholesterol	0 mg	Monounsaturated	0 g		

Sugar-Dusted Mocha Brownies

Serves 12

½ cup all-purpose flour
½ cup unsweetened cocoa powder
½ teaspoon baking powder
4 tablespoons light margarine (¼ cup)
1 tablespoon instant coffee crystals
1 cup sugar
Egg substitute equivalent to 2 eggs, or 2 eggs
¼ cup prune baby food
2 teaspoons vanilla
Vegetable oil spray
2 tablespoons powdered sugar

Preheat oven to 350° F.

In a small bowl, combine flour, cocoa powder, and baking powder. Set aside.

In a medium saucepan over medium-low heat, melt margarine. Add coffee crystals and stir until dissolved. Let cool slightly.

Add sugar, egg substitute, prune baby food, and vanilla to coffee mixture. Stir until well combined. Fold cocoa mixture into sugar mixture until well combined.

Spray an 8 × 8 × 2-inch cake pan with vegetable oil spray. Spoon batter into baking pan.

Bake, uncovered, for 18 to 20 minutes, or until a toothpick inserted near the center comes out almost clean (it should have a few fudgy crumbs on it).

Cool brownies in the pan on a wire rack. Sift powdered sugar over brownies.

Calories	124	Total Fat	2 g	Fiber	2 g
Protein	2 g	Saturated	1 g	Sodium	82 mg
Carbohydrate	25 g	Polyunsaturated	1 g		
Cholesterol	0 mg	Monounsaturated	1 g		

Chocolate Custard Cake with Raspberries

Serves 10

Vegetable oil spray

CAKE

14-ounce can nonfat sweetened condensed milk
Egg substitute equivalent to 5 eggs
½ cup fat-free milk
½ cup sugar
¼ cup unsweetened cocoa powder
¼ cup nonfat or low-fat chocolate syrup

1¼ cups seedless all-fruit raspberry preserves
10 ounces fresh or frozen raspberries, thawed
1 tablespoon powdered sugar (optional)

Preheat oven to 350° F. Spray an 8-inch nonstick round cake pan with vegetable oil spray. Cut a circle of parchment paper or wax paper to fit the bottom of the pan. Place paper in pan. If using wax paper, spray the top with vegetable oil spray.

In a large bowl, whisk together all cake ingredients. Pour into prepared pan.

Place the pan in the middle of a 12 x 17 x 1-inch jelly-roll pan and fill jelly-roll pan half full with warm water, or place cake pan in a baking pan (the bottom of a broiler pan works well) and add warm water to a depth of 1 inch.

Bake for 40 to 45 minutes, or until a toothpick inserted in the center of cake comes out clean. Remove cake pan from water and let cool on a wire rack for 10 minutes. Carefully invert onto a plate (it is not necessary to loosen sides first) and remove paper. Let cool for 15 minutes.

While cake is cooling, heat preserves in a small saucepan over low heat, stirring occasionally.

Top the cake with a thin coating of the preserves. Sprinkle with about half the raspberries. Cut the cake into 10 pie-shaped slices. Spoon remaining preserves on each dessert plate. Place each cake slice on preserves. Top with remaining raspberries, then dust lightly with powdered sugar.

For a more formal presentation, place raspberries in a ring around the top of the cake before cutting. Sprinkle any remaining berries on the dessert plates.

COOK'S TIP

This flanlike cake isn't a high riser—it doesn't contain any flour or leavening agent.

Calories	293	Total Fat	1 g	Fiber	5 g
Protein	8 g	Saturated	0 g	Sodium	103 mg
Carbohydrate	68 g	Polyunsaturated	0 g		
Cholesterol	2 mg	Monounsaturated	0 g		

Lemon Poppy Seed Cake

Serves 10

Vegetable oil spray
2 cups all-purpose flour
¾ cup sugar
1 tablespoon poppy seeds
2 teaspoons baking powder
¼ teaspoon baking soda
¼ teaspoon salt
¾ cup unsweetened applesauce (about 6 ounces)
1 teaspoon grated lemon rind
¼ cup fresh lemon juice (1 to 2 lemons)
2½ tablespoons acceptable vegetable oil
2 tablespoons corn syrup
1 teaspoon lemon extract
Whites of 4 eggs

Preheat oven to 350° F. Lightly spray a 9-inch round cake pan with vegetable oil spray. Set aside.

In a medium bowl, combine flour, sugar, poppy seeds, baking powder, baking soda, and salt. Set aside.

In another medium bowl, combine remaining ingredients except egg whites. Add to the flour mixture. Stir until just combined.

In a large bowl, beat the egg whites with an electric mixer until they form stiff peaks. Using a rubber scraper, fold the batter into the egg whites. Pour into the cake pan and smooth the top.

Bake for 30 minutes, or until a toothpick inserted in the center comes out clean. Cool in pan for 10 minutes, loosen sides of cake, and invert cake onto a cooling rack.

Calories	207	Total Fat	3 g	Fiber	1 g
Protein	4 g	Saturated	0 g	Sodium	217 mg
Carbohydrate	40 g	Polyunsaturated	2 g		
Cholesterol	0 mg	Monounsaturated	1 g		

Mango Brûlée with Pine Nuts

Serves 4

2 cups cubed fresh mango, papaya, or peaches (about
    3 mangoes, 2 medium papayas, or 4 medium
    peaches)
⅔ cup nonfat or low-fat sour cream
2 tablespoons pine nuts
2 tablespoons light brown sugar

Preheat broiler.
    Place fruit in the bottom of a 9-inch pie pan.
    Stir sour cream and dollop over fruit. Use the back of
a spoon to spread sour cream evenly.
    Sprinkle with pine nuts and brown sugar.
    Broil 4 to 6 inches from the heat for 1 to 2 minutes, or
until sugar melts and pine nuts toast (watch nuts closely
to avoid burning). Serve immediately.

COOK'S TIP

If fresh fruit is out of season, you can use frozen
unsweetened fruit that's been thawed, fruit in a jar, or
fruit canned in natural juice.

Calories	128	Total Fat	3 g	Fiber	2 g
Protein	4 g	Saturated	0 g	Sodium	47 mg
Carbohydrate	25 g	Polyunsaturated	1 g		
Cholesterol	1 mg	Monounsaturated	1 g		

Baked Apples

Serves 4

¼ cup port
¼ cup frozen unsweetened apple juice concentrate,
    thawed
¼ cup raisins or dried cranberries, blueberries, or tart
    cherries
¼ teaspoon ground cinnamon
4 baking apples, such as Rome Beauty, Jonathan, or
    McIntosh

Preheat oven to 350° F.

In a small saucepan over high heat, bring wine and juice concentrate to a boil. Turn heat off and add raisins and cinnamon. Stir, cover, and let sit for 15 minutes.

Meanwhile, core apples, but don't cut through the bottoms. If necessary, slice a small section from the bottom of each apple so that it does not fall over. With a paring knife, score around the apple, about ½ inch from the bottom. Peel from top down to scored line to prevent splitting.

Place apples in a glass baking dish so they are not touching. Fill centers with the juice-soaked raisins, spooning remaining juice evenly over apples. Pour water in the dish to a depth of ⅓ inch. Cover dish with aluminum foil. Bake for 20 minutes. Remove foil and bake for 20 minutes. Serve warm.

Calories	154	Total Fat	1 g	Fiber	4 g
Protein	1 g	Saturated	0 g	Sodium	6 mg
Carbohydrate	39 g	Polyunsaturated	0 g		
Cholesterol	0 mg	Monounsaturated	0 g		